HELEN GURLEY BROWN

The Queen
of
Cosmopolitan

Lucille Falkof

GEC GARRETT EDUCATIONAL CORPORATION

Cover: *Helen Gurley Brown. (Cosmopolitan* magazine.)

Manufactured in the United States of America

Edited and produced by Synthegraphics Corporation

Library of Congress Cataloging in Publication Data

Falkof, Lucille, 1924-
   Helen Gurley Brown : the queen of Cosmopolitan / Lucille Falkof.
     p. cm. — (Wizards of business)
   Includes index.
   Summary: A biography of Cosmopolitan Magazine's editor-in-chief, who is the author of several books and a television personality.
   ISBN 1-56074-013-2
   1. Brown, Helen Gurley.   2. Cosmopolitan (New York, N.Y. : 1952)—Juvenile literature.   3. Editors—United States—Biography—Juvenile literature.   4. Periodical editors—United States—Biography—Juvenile literature.   [1. Brown, Helen Gurley. 2. Editors.   3. Authors, American.]   I. Title.   II. Series.
PN149.9.B76F35   1992
070.4'1'092—dc20   91-32053
[B]   CIP
                                         AC

Contents

Chronology for *Helen Gurley Brown*

1922	Born on February 18 in Green Forest, Arkansas
1940-1942	Attended Woodbury Business College
1942-1948	Worked as a secretary for many companies in the entertainment business
1948-1958	Worked first as a secretary and later as a copywriter at Foote, Cone and Belding, an advertising agency
1956-1959	Received Francis Holmes Achievement Award for her outstanding work in advertising during these years
1959	Married David Brown on September 25
1962	Wrote bestseller, *Sex and the Single Girl*
1965	Became editor-in-chief of *Cosmopolitan* magazine
1972	Received a special award for editorial leadership from the American Newspaper Women's Club
1976-1981	Named by *World Almanac* as one of the twenty-five most influential women in the United States
1977	Received Distinguished Achievement Award in Journalism from Stanford University
1982	Published *Having It All*
1985	The Hearst Corporation endowed the Helen Gurley Brown professorship at Northwestern University's Medill School of Journalism
1990	Celebrated 25 years as editor-in-chief of *Cosmopolitan* magazine

Chapter 1

A Cause for Celebration

It could not have been a more perfect evening. From the huge windows, one could see the last rosy hues of the setting sun sparkling on the Hudson River and the palisades of New Jersey. But the real attraction was inside the Rainbow Room, the celebrated ballroom atop Rockefeller Center in the heart of New York City. The huge room glowed with lights and the reflections of sequined gowns and sparkling diamond and gold jewelry.

It was June 25, 1990, and the star of this evening was a tiny, slender lady named Helen Gurley Brown. Movie stars and famed television personalities, opera stars and writers, financiers and ambassadors had all come to pay tribute on the occasion of Helen Gurley Brown's twenty-fifth anniversary as editor-in-chief of *Cosmopolitan* magazine.

THE CENTER OF ATTENTION

Clad in a short-skirted pink, fluffy dress, created by famed dress designer Bill Blass, a smiling Helen Gurley Brown was the center of attention. She floated through the room greeting her guests. One of them was TV personality Barbara Walters, who had interviewed Helen and her husband, David Brown, in their palatial apartment facing Central Park in New York. Even the U.S. Ambassador to Canada, Edward Ney, and his wife, Judy, had crossed the border to attend the party, despite a crisis in the Canadian government.

It was even rumored that former Presidents Jimmy Carter and Richard Nixon would be there. "It's too bad they're not because I love them both dearly," said Helen.

Beaming at his wife's guests and just as proud of his wife's accomplishments as ever was David Brown. As an author as well as a producer of Broadway plays and Hollywood films, David Brown was a celebrity in his own right.

Driven by Fear

But tonight was Helen's night. Photographers and reporters from magazines and newspapers all over the country tried to get "one more picture" or a comment or two from the guest of honor. One journalist asked, "Mrs. Brown, what is the secret of your success in a business where magazines come and go and editors come and go even quicker?"

"Fear," she replied, "I get up every morning very nervous that I'm going to lose my job."

People around her at that moment may have laughed, but Helen Brown was deadly serious in her comment. Fear of failing was one of the many things that had driven this woman from small villages in the Ozark Mountains of Arkansas to become one of the 25 most influential women in the United States.

There is little doubt that anyone can ever see Helen Gurley Brown's life as anything but a smashing success story. She is not only the **editor** of one of the country's most successful magazines, she is also the author of several books and a TV personality. And in the course of her work, she travels *first class* all over the world. The little girl from Arkansas has come a long, long way.

Chapter 2

From Dreamer to Doer

At a very early age, Helen Gurley knew she wanted more out of life than what she saw around her. She didn't like her hillbilly cousins, who went around saying "ain't" and "cain't" and "she give me five dollars for that hat." Helen knew that they were good people who led honorable lives, but from the time she was seven years old, she knew she wanted to separate herself from their world.

Helen was born on February 18, 1922, in Green Forest, Arkansas, the second daughter of Ira and Cleo Gurley. Both parents were school teachers. Helen has written little about her early years, but she does remember certain things from those days.

By 1930, the country was suffering from the **Great Depression.** It was a time when jobs were hard to find and

4

those who were fortunate to have jobs worked for low wages. But Helen remembers that even with all the hardships, clothes were very important to her family. Her mother sewed beautifully and managed to make sure that her girls always had a Sunday School dress, an Easter dress, new school outfits and costumes for class plays. That love of clothes, and a feeling that one must always try to look one's best, have continued through all of Helen's life.

A FAMILY TRAGEDY

When she was ten years old, tragedy struck Helen's family. Ira Gurley was killed in a freak elevator accident. Looking back on those years, Helen described the effect his death had on her.

She remembers her father as a very affectionate man who enjoyed being with his daughters and with whom she had wonderful times. As a result of his death, Helen has always been afraid of losing the strong men in her life – her employer and her husband – the way she lost her father, the first important man in her life.

The Lonely Years

Life changed dramatically for Helen after her father's death. Her mother was not a strong woman and found it difficult to get on with her life. It was perhaps for this reason that the little family moved into Helen's grandmother's home in Osage, Arkansas, a tiny town with a population of 40 people.

Helen remembers sitting under the stars at age twelve

with her sister, Mary. The two girls would read magazines like *Photoplay* and *Silver Screen* and dream about life in Hollywood. Hollywood seemed as far away as Mars, yet Helen dates the beginnings of her intense "drive" to get ahead to the longing and the lonesomeness of her life during those years.

Part of Helen's life at this time involved the world of make-believe. She loved to create things and to act in school plays. But her mother stressed the importance of achievement and would reward her accomplishments. Helen responded by working hard and managed to get A's in grade school.

During Helen's teenage years, the three Gurleys moved to Los Angeles, where they lived by a railroad track. The trains passing by would make such a racket that no one could talk. Helen also remembers that the floor of her bedroom was wobbly because gophers used to tunnel up under it.

By this time the Great Depression was ending. The three women, like so many of the people who flooded the Los Angeles area, hoped to start a new life. But once again, tragedy struck. At age nineteen, Helen's sister, Mary, became ill with polio, a terrible paralyzing disease, and was confined to a wheelchair for the rest of her life.

Lessons from a Memorable Teacher

Despite her sister's illness, Helen has some good memories of her high school years. It was at John H. Francis Polytechnic High School in 1939 that Helen met a wonderful English teacher, Ethel McGhee. Miss McGhee gave encouragement and support to the skinny little high school student. She helped

Helen to appreciate the beauty of language and words, both in reading and writing. Miss McGhee coached Helen and helped her to win a public-speaking contest.

Ethel McGhee also gave Helen her first lesson on how to shake hands. One day, a dean from an important woman's college in Los Angeles visited the classroom and shook hands with several of the students. Later, Ethel commented to Helen that the dean had said Helen gave a handshake "like a wet fish." Ethel told Helen that she should grasp a person's hand firmly and act like she was *glad* to meet the person. Helen Brown has done that ever since and has passed on the lesson to other young women she meets.

STARTING OUT

In 1940, at age eighteen, Helen enrolled at Woodbury Business College to learn shorthand and typing. While still attending Woodbury, she got her first job, as secretary to an announcer at radio station KHJ in Los Angeles. The pay was six dollars a week. Helen worked furiously to learn typing and shorthand, but the job did not last long. The announcer turned out to be a screamer, who constantly reminded Helen of some idiotic thing she had done.

There was never any question but that Helen would have to work. From her wheelchair, Mary earned forty cents an hour by telephoning people for the C.E. Hooper Rating Service to find out what radio show they were listening to. Mrs. Gurley pinned tickets on merchandise in the marketing room at Sears Roebuck. The family could not have managed if Helen had not finally obtained a job for which she was paid eighteen dollars a week.

Learning the Hard Way

Before she was in her mid-twenties, Helen was already working at her sixth job. Looking back on those years, Helen admits freely that she was hardly a valuable **employee.** She would call in sick and sneak down to the beach, then arrive at work the next day with her arms smeared with milk of magnesia so she would look as if she was "diseased."

It took Helen several years to realize that she had to give herself wholeheartedly to her work in order to get ahead. She clearly remembers one incident when she failed to make the most of an opportunity.

On Sunday, December 7, 1941, the U.S. naval base at Pearl Harbor, in Hawaii, was attacked by the Japanese. The other secretary at radio station KHJ, where Helen worked at the time, heard the news and rushed to the station to see if she could be of any help. It turned out to be one of the most momentous events in radio history.

Helen also heard the news, but she had no idea where Pearl Harbor was or that the attack would involve the United States in World War II. Besides, it was Sunday, so Helen turned over in bed and went back to sleep.

For her efforts, the on-the-job secretary, Mary Ellen, received a raise and was driven around town in a limousine for a month. Helen, on the other hand, learned a lesson she has never forgotten.

When Glamour Isn't Enough

At one point, Helen worked for the Abbott and Costello radio show as a script girl. But she was hardly a dependable addition to the staff. She loved being in the same building with so many celebrities and could not resist running across the hall to see such stars as Bing Crosby rehearse his show.

One day, Helen's boss asked her to make a list of all the sound-effect props needed for the show that week. (For a radio show, sound effects help the listener to imagine what action is taking place.) Helen forgot the three most important props — crunching gravel, a squeaky door, and a nail to be hammered into a piece of wood. Another time, she forgot to notify the guest star when a rehearsal was called off. Imagine the fuss that took place when the star arrived and no one was there to greet her!

Although Helen loved being part of the glamourous entertainment business, she still had not yet learned the keys to success. It was not until she was working at her seventeenth job that she began to realize what she would have to do to succeed in business. She also learned what to do when one is fired from a job — begin to look for another job immediately.

AT LAST – THE RIGHT BOSS

By this time, Helen knew that her secretarial skills were never going to be the greatest, that she would never find a movie star to date, and that she had better settle for a job in a less glamourous business. It proved to be the turning point in her career, for her attitude towards work now changed.

In 1948, Helen went to work as a secretary for Donald Belding at the advertising firm of Foote, Cone and Belding. She found her boss to be quite kind, and he and his wife even adopted Helen socially. They would invite her to parties at their home and take her to social events. In return, Helen was determined to be a hard worker. It took an hour on a bus to get to work, and it might still be dark outside when she arrived. Nevertheless, Helen was in the office every morning to greet her employer. She did not stop for coffee breaks or even take the time to chat with other secretaries during lunch hours.

Helen began to realize that she was not only earning a good salary but she was also learning new things about business. To this day, Helen sees being a secretary as a good way of getting ahead, even for college graduates. You can get into the business world at a higher level, you deal with executives, and, if you are clever, you can eavesdrop and learn a lot. To prove her point, four of Helen's secretaries have moved on to editorial positions at *Cosmopolitan* magazine.

At one point while working for Don Belding, Helen decided to enter a magazine contest sponsored by *Glamour* magazine. The subject was "Ten Girls with Taste," and the prize was a trip to Hawaii and a new wardrobe.

"I had about as much taste as a giraffe," she says, "but I could write pretty well. And I was one of their ten winners. On the questionnaire it said, 'What are your goals?' . . . So I said I wanted to be a **copywriter.**"

From Secretary to Copywriter

As a result of that comment, Mr. Belding gave Helen an opportunity to write Sunkist radio commercials once a year. It was not always easy to figure out what to say to a housewife so that she would not switch the dial during a commercial. But after each copywriting job for Sunkist, Helen would go back to being a secretary.

Helen credits her success with her ability to "feel what people want." She would write entertaining letters to her boss when he was out of town on business. Instinctively, she knew what to write that would please him, and she always included a little office gossip. Even Don Belding's wife enjoyed her letters. One day, she suggested to Don that Helen be given an opportunity to write copy full-time. Finally, after five years as Belding's secretary, she became a full-time copywriter.

THE MOUSEBURGER

Helen was now thirty-one years old. She had thirteen years of experience under her belt and had finished her seventeenth secretarial job. She had achieved some success but was still unsure about herself or her abilities. She was still, in her own words, "a mouseburger." Yet, she must have been doing very well in her work for she was given the Francis Holmes Achievement Award for outstanding work in advertising for the years 1956–59.

Later, Helen would write books about the kind of person, like herself, who has the drive to make a success of herself. In her book, *Having It All,* written in 1982, Helen describes mouseburgers as people who have a normal I.Q. but are not particularly attractive, may lack a good education or a good family background, who lack confidence but have drive, and who *can* make something of themselves if they work hard at it.

Helen was now working hard, and it was beginning to pay off. By living economically, she was able to put aside a week's salary each month to send to her mother and sister, who had moved back to Little Rock, Arkansas. Then, in 1958, another ad agency stole her away from Foote, Cone and Belding. She was given twice the salary and the prestigious Max Factor cosmetics account.

Life was beginning to look pretty good, but there was still one thing missing. Although Helen had enjoyed many dates and even several romances, there was still no "special" person in her life. But this, too, was about to change.

Chapter 3

Enter David Brown

To this day, Helen insists it was a cloud-gray Mercedes Benz that won her a husband. She had finally saved enough money to treat herself to something she had always wanted. The other item she now wanted was a husband. She was thirty-six years old and felt ready for marriage.

David Brown was a vice-president of production at a movie company when Helen first met him briefly at a party. Although she thought he was attractive, she also knew he was married. Later, when Helen heard that David had been divorced, she asked a friend, Ruth Schandorf, to introduce her to David again. They then met at a dinner party that Ruth arranged.

A LOVE MATCH

At the time, David Brown had been a journalist, a managing editor at *Cosmopolitan* magazine, and was now a vice-president at Twentieth Century Fox, a movie company. He was impressive, charming, and well paid, and Helen found herself falling in love.

At the end of the evening, David escorted her to her car. As he opened the door of her cloud-gray Mercedes Benz, Helen managed to tell him that she had bought the car for herself *with cash*. As Helen describes the impression that statement made: "I've never doubted that I eventually persuaded him to marry me because he had never known a girl who paid all cash for a pair of *stockings,* let alone a sports car."

This was a time when most women did not work or earn enough to buy their own cars. David must have been impressed because he began to date Helen regularly. For over a year, David courted her. But having been through two divorces, he was not in any hurry to get married again. Helen tried to play it cool and be patient.

The Reluctant Groom

But one evening, after dinner at David's home, the housekeeper brought out some samples of draperies she had selected for the house. Helen realized that if he was letting his housekeeper make the selection, he was not thinking of getting married.

That night, Helen told David that since he had no intention of getting married, she was not going to see him again. It took several days, but David finally called Helen and said something like, "I surrender." But getting him to the altar was not all that easy.

After breaking several dates for the wedding, David

Helen Gurley Brown with her husband, David Brown, on an evening out on the town. (UPI/Bettmann.)

called Helen one Thursday afternoon in September of 1959. "I'm ready," he said. Helen did not hesitate for a moment. No one was told except David's secretary and his son by a former marriage. David merely told people he would be out of the office. It was hardly the romantic wedding of which Helen had dreamed, but she has never regretted her decision.

Helen and David have been married for more than thirty years. Each of them has openly discussed their marriage in books they have written. What comes out loud and clear is that this is a couple who are good for each other. They share mutual interests, and each is proud of the other's success.

CURE FOR BOREDOM

Helen might have resigned from her job after her marriage, as most women did at that time, but she decided to stay on. However, she was not finding her work as a copywriter very fulfilling. She worked hard at her assignments, and her copy was seen by all of the right people in the advertising agency, but none of her work became copy in magazines or newspapers. In addition, there were two other women copywriters at the agency who had the same assignments.

One day, as Helen and David were taking their regular Sunday walk in Will Rogers State Park in West Los Angeles, she began to talk about her feelings. She had been working for twenty years and was disappointed that no one at the agency seemed to appreciate her work. She was bored. David had helped other people write books. Perhaps he could help her. Did he have any ideas?

Casually, David mentioned an idea that he had outlined and recently given to a woman writer. However, the woman had not shown any interest in using the idea. Helen listened to David's description of the book and immediately felt that the subject was something she could write about. After all, it had to do with working women and certainly Helen, with her seventeen jobs and many years of experience, was well qualified to write on the subject! David managed to get the outline back from the woman to whom he had given it, and thereupon Helen began a new career.

A Smashing Success

Helen began by making notes while under the hair dryer in her little office at Kenyon and Eckhardt, the advertising agency where she was working. As the ideas began to flow, she created a new outline and then began the actual writing. As Helen describes it, without having a built-in editor (David) in the house, the book might never have gotten off the ground. She would write a chapter and David would edit it, always explaining why something didn't work and how to fix it. Then she would begin again.

Finally, in the fifth draft, Helen found her own style. She wrote simply about her own experiences, what kind of woman she was, that she was married later than most women, but that it was right for her.

At that time, a woman's success depended on how successful her husband was. If a woman was unmarried and over thirty, it was assumed she must be an unattracitve spinster. Helen's idea that a woman could be over thirty, have a successful career, and still be attractive to men was a shocking idea for its day. It took her a year to write the book, *Sex and the Single Girl,* for she was still working at Kenyon and Eckhardt during the day.

The first **publisher** to see the final draft of the book was an old friend, and Helen was in tears when he turned it down. She was sobbing so hard that she did not even hear the suggestion he made for another publisher. That publisher's name was Bernard Geis, who sent Helen an acceptance and an advance for six thousand dollars ten days after seeing the manuscript.

The book was published in 1962 and became an instant success, climbing to the top of the best-seller list. It was published in 35 countries and in almost as many languages.

The New Celebrity

Helen Gurley Brown was now a celebrity. She was asked to appear on the *Today Show* and became a regular on the *Johnny Carson Show*. She made more money than she had ever dreamed of, received bushels of mail, and quit her job.

Even though David was in the motion picture industry, he had never thought of making Helen's book into a movie. But Jack Warner, head of Warner Brothers Studios, did. The movie was made with Henry Fonda and Tony Curtis, and Natalie Wood played the role of Helen Gurley Brown.

And then David Brown was fired by Twentieth Century Fox. He had been instrumental in bringing *Cleopatra* to the screen, the film that starred Elizabeth Taylor and Richard Burton, and had a cast of thousands. The movie had cost the studio so much to produce that it was a financial disaster. Now David was out of a job.

NEW BEGINNINGS

However, David soon found another position, to start a new **hardcover** division for the New American Library publishing company. That meant moving to New York City, where Helen tried to find things to keep her busy.

She wrote a new book, *Sex and the Office.* It sold fifty thousand copies in hardcover, but it was not quite the same success as her first book. She tried her hand at writing a newspaper column for the *Los Angeles Times* **Syndicate** and found that she was good at it. She spent hours answering the huge amount of mail that she received. Women enjoyed her frank and honest comments and wrote to her for advice as to an older sister. But Helen Brown had become a **workaholic** and needed more than a newspaper column to keep herself busy.

It was David who came up with an idea. One afternoon, seeing the pile of letters awaiting her, David commented, "You know, there are all these women out there who trust and need you. You ought to have a magazine."

Out of that comment was born Helen Gurley Brown's long and successful association with *Cosmopolitan* magazine.

Chapter 4

Taking Charge at Cosmo

"The difference between David and me and some other people with ideas is that we sit down and do it." For Helen and David Brown, that comment sums up their **philosophy** and serves as their explanation as to why some people are successful and others are not.

When David suggested to her the idea of starting a magazine, Helen had never even worked on one. But after David suggested she try developing a magazine, the creative juices began flowing. Both of them thought up dozens of ideas for articles. It was Helen who decided that the magazine should be designed for women who were not living only through their husbands and children, but who wanted to do something on their own.

Helen knew enough about magazine publishing to know

it was advertising that pays for a large part of the publication costs. Her experience as a copywriter made her knowledgeable about the needs of advertisers. So one of the first things she did was to sit down and make a list of all the products that might be advertised in her kind of magazine. Together, she and David prepared a neatly typed **prospectus.** They decided to call the magazine *Femme,* the French word for "woman." They would later learn that a magazine using that very same name already existed in France. It did not really matter, however, because what they ended up doing was not to start a new magazine, but to revive a dying old one.

When a Market Changes

Some business people do not look at future trends as they operate their companies. They stick with what they have been producing rather than recognizing that their market is changing. One example is that of wagon-makers, who continued to make wagons long after the automobile was a common sight on American highways. Those who switched to making automobile bodies continued in business. Other companies failed.

By the 1960s, the new technology of television was well perfected. Most homes had at least one set, and television was beginning to affect all phases of American life. More and more people were turning to television for entertainment and to get instant news about such events as the war in Vietnam. A wealth of new ideas about the country and the American culture were being talked about.

Advertisers, aware of these and new trends, began moving their dollars from the printed page to television commercials. Helen and David Brown's idea of focusing on a particular audience, the working woman, was the wave of the future. Many general magazines did not take these changes into account and failed. New publications took their place, magazines that catered to a segment of the population with a particular interest, such as the sports fan or people interested in health or the environment.

ENTER THE HEARST CORPORATION

David Brown had connections in the magazine field from his days at *Pic, Liberty,* and *Cosmopolitan* magazines. It was only logical that he should take the simple paste-up dummy (sample) of *Femme* magazine to a number of people he knew. After being turned down by several companies, he struck gold at a luncheon at Sardi's East, a popular meeting place for the literary and Broadway crowd. While chatting with a friend, Jack O'Connell, David asked what was new in the Hearst Corporation, parent company of *Cosmopolitan* and many other publications.

In his book, *Let Me Entertain You,* Brown describes the incident. Jack said, "They're desperate about *Cosmopolitan.* It looks as though they may fold it. But they're taking one more shot." David's ears perked up, especially when Jack told him they were hoping to change the magazine format and look for an audience of single career women who were not into child-rearing or PTAs. At that point, a bell rang in David's head.

He remembered that Bernard Geis, the publisher of Helen's book, *Sex and the Single Girl,* knew the president of Hearst Magazines, Richard Deems. When Brown called Geis and explained about the new magazine that Helen was in-terested in doing, Geis offered to get the material into Deems' hands. Within hours, David received a call that Deems was interested. At that point, Helen began to have some second thoughts about the project.

As Helen tells the story in David's book, *Let Me Enter-tain You,* "I wasn't absolutely sure that I ought to be a maga-zine editor. (It's like telling you to go be an astronaut or a brain surgeon — something you simply had never done before. Al-though it was challenging, you weren't sure (a) that you wanted to or (b) that you could do it.)"

But things had already begun to move quickly. By the following evening, Helen and David were in the Deems' apart-ment in the Waldorf Towers, a hotel in New York City. While Helen sat in a corner, worried and nervous about such a big undertaking, David **negotiated** the contract. Before she had time to think, Helen was being interviewed by the Hearst pub-licity people for their **press release.** The die was cast. Helen Gurley Brown was now the new editor-in-chief of *Cosmopoli-tan* magazine.

THE FIRST DAYS AT COSMO

What Helen Brown had inherited was a seventy-nine year-old magazine. It had once been a popular and successful magazine that had carried stories by such famous authors as Somerset Maugham. Now the publication was dying and the Hearst Corporation looked to Helen Brown to turn the aging magazine around.

Strong women, such as feminists, are not usually considered crybabies. But Helen Brown admits publicly that she is both a feminist and a crybaby. The night before her first day of work at *Cosmopolitan* (hereafter to be called *Cosmo*, the nickname used by the staff and its editor-in-chief), Helen was walking down Park Avenue, sobbing.

She had a feeling of being abandoned, of being thrown to the wolves. After all, when they had first discussed the idea of a magazine, David was thinking of himself as the publisher. He would have been there daily, to support her, to tell her how to begin. In the meantime, he had taken on a new job with Twentieth Century Fox. Helen was on her own.

By the morning of her first day of work, Helen was feeling a bit better. She dressed herself carefully in a pretty, soft wool jersey dress with a ruffle at the hem. Just before leaving for work, she turned to David and asked, "Just what do I do when I get there?" His reply was, "Ask the managing editor to lunch."

Things did not quite work out as planned. The managing editor already had a date for lunch and then quit within the week. Helen would later learn that unhappy staff members mumbled that she should have learned something about

This is the first photograph taken of Helen Gurley Brown as she began her career at Cosmopolitan *in March 1965. (Cosmopolitan magazine.)*

the magazine business before being given the top job. And it was true. Before undertaking the assignment, Helen had never worked on a magazine, had never edited other people's copy, and had never been an **administrator.** There was no doubt that it took real nerve for a person with no experience to come into a new industry as a top executive.

But Helen Gurley Brown was wise enough to ask for the schedule for future issues and discovered that there was no schedule. She looked at the drab and uninteresting issues due to come out in May and June and decided to let them go. July would be "her" issue, and she began to make plans for the changes she had in mind.

The November 19, 1965, issue of Life *magazine showed Helen winning big smiles from the staff of* Cosmopolitan. *The staff was beginning to learn that her southern charm did not hide her strong executive ability.* (Walter Daran, *Life* magazine © Time Warner Inc.)

David recalls that Helen would phone him almost every afternoon, frantically in need of help. "Can you meet me in a taxi outside the Hearst building?" she would ask.

The staff needed decisions to be made, and Helen needed help. While they rode around town in a taxi, Helen would pull out a stack of papers and the two of them would go over page proofs, cover **blurbs,** and ideas for articles. At night, she would bring home as many manuscripts and schedules as she could stuff into her briefcase and the process would be repeated.

One of Helen's chores was to work out payment with the authors of the stories and articles that appeared in the magazine. Her natural tendency to be tight with money helped her to become a tough negotiator in setting prices for their work.

Settling In

In the beginning, Helen enjoyed assigning articles to authors, but over the years, she has let others do that chore. David offered to help her with all the fiction manuscripts. Sometimes they would make selections while riding around in a taxi. David would tell her which articles to buy, which ones to forget, and which needed editing.

Helen has found that her biggest task, and the one she enjoys most, is reading and editing the many manuscripts that come into the *Cosmo* office. At first, David would check her editing, showing her what worked and at times telling her that she had edited so much that she had taken the life out of the article. These days, she tries to save her Saturdays and Sundays to edit manuscripts and has grown to love it.

David edits the monthly column that Helen writes for the magazine. It is called "Step into My Parlor." For some reason, she finds this monthly chore a real challenge. Helen has learned that when ideas do not flow, she is better off putting aside her column and tackling an editing job. As the editing begins to give her a feeling of success, she can then put that aside and go back to her column. Helen finds that this routine works best for her and does not lose time fretting when words won't come.

CASH RESULTS

The new *Cosmo* took off like a rocket. From July 1965 on, sales increased every month. This was a time when general interest magazines and radio were having a hard time competing with the new media star, television. Helen Gurley Brown had targeted her magazine for an audience that she knew and understood well — the new career woman — and the results were fantastic.

What was new about the magazine? What did it include that made it so successful? Why has it continued to be successful for the past twenty-five years?

Chapter 5

Recognition and Rewards

Helen Gurley Brown IS the *Cosmo* girl. It was easy for her to know what her audience of readers wants because she gives them the things that she wanted twenty-five years ago for herself . . . and still wants today. *Cosmopolitan* magazine was not to be a magazine for the stay-at-home housewife. It would not include fancy recipes for exotic dishes that took two hours to prepare, or suggestions for children's birthday parties or hand-crafted Christmas presents. This was to be a magazine for the young, adventurous woman who was willing and capable of working her way to the top.

CHANGING AN IMAGE

Brown realized that she had to change the image of the magazine quickly, and what better way to do it than to do something dramatic with the cover. A few months before Helen took over the magazine, the cover showed a picture of a nurse in uniform. It was neither dramatic nor particularly attractive. So one of the first things she did was to call Francesco Scavullo, a fashion photographer who had a reputation for making beautiful women look *more* beautiful.

Helen hired Scavullo on the spot, and he has continued to create the beautiful and dramatic *Cosmo* covers that decorate the newsstands of the world. For years, women's magazines had featured on their covers the cake you could learn how to bake by following the instructions inside. Now, the *Cosmopolitan* cover featured the kind of woman *you* could be if you followed the instructions inside the magazine.

A Formula for Success

Cosmo was one of the first magazines to target its contents for a particular group . . . the young career woman. This is what people in industry call **niche marketing.** The magazine offered to the working woman the high fashion and beauty approach of a magazine like *Glamour,* along with stories written by such popular authors as Rona Jaffe. But it geared its articles to the concerns of the young woman interested in making a career for herself.

Other magazines have entered the field, trying to appeal to the same group of women, but Helen Gurley Brown and *Cosmo* have managed to stay far ahead of the newcomers. *Cosmo* has continued to be successful because its editor-in-chief believes in the product she is selling.

Today, the bulk of *Cosmo's* readers are women between ages eighteen and thirty-four. According to its publisher, Seth E. Hoyt, almost three-fourths of the readers work full-time, and thirty-five percent are college educated.

After five years as editor-in-chief at Cosmo, *Helen Gurley Brown felt very much at home in her New York office.* (Cosmopolitan magazine.)

GIVING THE AUDIENCE WHAT IT WANTS

Cosmopolitan still contains such things as cooking recipes, but they are recipes for the career girl who arrives home late from the office and has to put a simple but elegant and nutritious dinner on the table. There are fashion and beauty hints for the woman who wants to be in the latest style but who does not have hours to spend shopping or in a beauty parlor.

That was the image of what has come to be called "The *Cosmo* Girl." Helen had a very clear image of that girl. "She was me, 20 years earlier, the girl with her nose pressed to the glass. . . . The only way up was to work at it, to do it." Though now a woman in her late 60s, Helen Gurley Brown still sees herself as that girl.

There are critics who have been irked by Mrs. Brown's use of the term "girl," finding it demeaning to mature women. For those critics, Helen has an answer. "As long as men take no offense in being addressed as 'Old Boy,' revel in being part of 'The Old Boy Network' or called a 'Good Old Boy,' we see no reason not to call a girl a girl regardless of age."

IMPACT OF THE FEMINIST MOVEMENT

The early 1960s saw not only the rise of Helen Gurley Brown as a celebrity, they also witnessed the rise of a new feminist movement. Spurred on by Betty Friedan's book, *The Feminine Mystique*, published in 1963, women began organizing for greater equality with men in the workplace as well as in the home.

Cosmopolitan was hardly militant in urging political change or pushing for laws to guarantee greater equality between the sexes. It did encourage women, particularly single women, to become more independent and assertive in earning money and building a career. No longer were women to be identified only in their roles as wife and mother. Whether single or married, they also had earned a place in the working world.

On the other hand, *Cosmo* did not play down the importance of love in a person's life. While the superfeminist almost denied the need to be attractive, *Cosmo* urged women to be both hard-working AND attractive. *Cosmo* and Helen Brown believe that any woman can be attractive, and being attractive is one way to move up the business ladder.

The Feminists Attack

Such ideas did not always sit well with the leaders of the feminist movement. One editor of a women's magazine labeled the *Cosmo* girl "the liberated ideal." But other women felt differently. A college professor complained that the *Cosmopolitan* girl idea treated women as "sedentary objects."

In 1970, several activists in the feminist movement, including Kate Millett, Robin Morgan, and Ti-Grace Atkinson, held a sit-in at the offices of *Cosmopolitan*. Helen remembers when Kate Millett strode into her office. Mrs. Brown is a slight person, weighing not quite 100 pounds, so Ms. Millett's approach must have been a bit overwhelming. With a pixyish smile, Helen recalls the event, "I was backed up against the radiator . . . but it wasn't very hot."

The feminists were angered by many of *Cosmo's* articles on "How to Find a Man." Other feminists were annoyed that *Cosmo,* with such a large circulation aimed at a female audience, did not take a more politically active role in its pages.

One journalist, Karen Durbin, said, "On the one hand, the magazine has a lively sense of women being kept from their birthright. But it has no political understanding of how that's happened. Even worse, it doesn't even seem interested."

Helen Brown has more than once been asked whether she feels she has led American women to liberation. Her answer: "No, I'm only trying to report what's going on out there." Yet Mrs. Brown sees herself as a "devout feminist."

> My own definition is that a feminist believes in equality for men and women . . . a woman should be free to develop every facet of her life and talent without interference. But I also think a feminist should accept it if a woman doesn't want to realize her potential.

Feminists may also be annoyed by the fact that Helen never hesitates to give credit to her husband, David Brown, for the original ideas he gave her for her first book and the new look of *Cosmo.*

A Change of Mind

For years, it has troubled Helen that women's groups were so critical of her. She cannot understand why some people think there is something terribly wrong with a woman who enjoys being a girl. Many of her former critics have changed their minds about *Cosmo.* Betty Friedan has become a fan because of *Cosmo's* support for such feminist subjects as the need for husband and wife to share home duties and government or corporate help with child care. Gloria Steinem, another ardent feminist, even wrote an article for *Cosmo's* twentieth anniversary issue.

The Women's Liberation Movement

When Helen Gurley Brown took over as editor-in-chief of *Cosmopolitan* in 1965, the first rumblings of the present feminist movement, called "women's liberation," were beginning in the United States. Originally called "feminism," women's liberation is a social movement that aims to give women equal status with men.

Though many young people think the feminist movement is a new one, it is not. It began in western Europe in the 1700s. The early feminists sought equal education with men, the right to own property, and the right to vote. Over the years, many of these goals were achieved in the United States.

Today, the women's liberation movement calls for equal job opportunities, equal salaries, and equality in sports. It also seeks to liberate women by giving them the freedom to make their own decisions about their careers and life-styles. As a result of this movement, there are now more professional opportunities

> open to women, more women's sport teams, and more day care centers so women who are mothers can also hold jobs.
>
> The rise of the new feminism occurred at the same time that Helen Gurley Brown decided to develop a magazine that would appeal to the new career woman. Both events helped to account for the success of *Cosmopolitan.*

THE ADVERTISERS' POINT OF VIEW

The companies that advertised in *Cosmo* cared little about the magazine's stand on the feminist movement. What they cared most about was getting their money's worth from the large sums they spent to advertise in the magazine. One pleased advertiser felt that active and self-reliant women aspired to become like the *Cosmo* girl. That, in turn, made it easier for marketing people to sell their products to these women. Helen and David Brown had been right on target when they had planned their prospectus for advertisers. The results paid off almost immediately.

When Mrs. Brown took over at *Cosmo,* the magazine's monthly **circulation** was 783,000 copies and falling. Today, it is bought monthly by 2.7 million American women. Its closest competitors, *Glamour* and Mademoiselle, reach 2.2 million and 1.2 million readers, respectively. It is one of the five largest-selling magazines in the country.

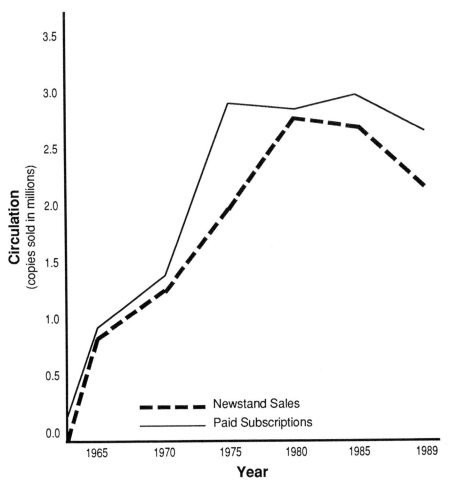

Sales figures show the dramatic increase in both newstand sales and paid subscriptions since Helen Brown took over at Cosmopolitan *in 1965.*

According to publisher Seth Hoyt, *Cosmo* readers are "young and indulgent . . . terrifically interesting people if you are trying to sell something." And advertisers want to sell their products. The greater the circulation, the greater the number of women who see the ads. In 1965, advertising filled 354 pages and brought $1.5 million dollars to *Cosmopolitan*. To-day, advertising has increased to 2,352 pages and brings in

revenue of $125 million. The greater the advertising revenues, the greater the profits for the magazine.

In 1990, Helen celebrated the twenty-fifth anniversary of her appointment as editor-in-chief of *Cosmopolitan* magazine. The twenty-fifth anniversary issue was the largest *Cosmopolitan* ever published. Stories about Helen Gurley Brown's role in the magazine's success appeared in many newspapers and business magazines.

COSMO'S *MORE SERIOUS SIDE*

As the years have gone by, *Cosmo* has not hesitated to include articles of a serious nature. The editors have discovered that one of the powerful urges of *Cosmo* readers has been their desire to learn. There have been articles dealing with such serious subjects as **finance,** women's rights, and abortion. The magazine has also included interviews with well-known political figures.

In a recent issue, the cover blurb read "The Big Fight in the Women's Movement. Will It Set Back Feminism?" In that case, there was no question that such a serious article warranted use of the term "woman," not "girl."

GOING INTERNATIONAL

Today, *Cosmo* can be read in at least a dozen different languages, from Japanese and Spanish to French and German, in twenty-three foreign editions. The expanded *Cosmo* em-

At the office, Helen Gurley Brown keeps her staff and herself working at a fast pace. (Harry Benson.)

pire keeps Mrs. Brown busy, for she serves as the editorial director of all foreign-language versions. Each of the foreign magazines deals with some but not all of the subjects of the American version. This is because each of the foreign magazines contains what is appropriate for the culture and the audience of the country in which it is published.

Several times a year Helen travels abroad to make new connections and to check on *Cosmo's* overseas publications. Despite the differences in culture, there are certain features in the magazine that remain constant, even in the foreign publications. A beautiful woman is sure to grace the cover, and there are blurbs that tell the important contents in the issue.

Usually, the cover girls are models, but on occasion, the American publication has featured such well-known women as Jacqueline Kennedy Onassis, Elizabeth Taylor, and Cher. For the twenty-fifth anniversary issue, the cover girl was Madonna. Brown prefers not to feature movie stars or other public personalities on *Cosmo's* cover. They are harder to fit into a production schedule, and she then gets calls from other well-known women asking to be considered for a cover.

Helen treats all of her editors as her daughters. (The only man is the editor of the Japanese edition.) "I have no children of my own," she says, "so I think of *these* as my children."

In an interview in 1985, Helen explained what she thinks is the basis of her success. "The reason *Cosmo* works is that underneath all this there is only . . . *me,* being . . . totally, *totally* sincere.

Chapter 6

Having It All

If Helen Gurley Brown ever had any doubts about her success, the celebration of her twenty-five years as editor-in-chief of *Cosmo* should have reassured her. Magazines and newspapers featured long background stories on her life and career. Business publications have called her one of the top ten women in the field of business. The June 1990 issue of *Vanity* magazine featured a nine-page article on the life and times of "The Mouseburger." What is life really like for this great lady of the publishing industry?

A DAY IN THE LIFE OF HELEN GURLEY BROWN

"Before 8 o'clock is the middle of the night — I feel ill if I get up before then. I have seen the sun rise and I know it's beautiful out there, but I can't get up." But at the crack of eight, Helen's day begins – with an hour of serious exercise.

Until age forty-seven, exercise was the farthest thing from Helen Brown's mind. She explains that she was such a skinny, sickly youngster as a fourteen-year-old at Belmont High School in Los Angeles that she took "rest" while other kids took gym. But by her senior year, she was strong enough to attempt basketball. However, when she finally got her hands on the ball, she found herself facing a screaming team. She was aiming the ball at the opposition's basket!

Although Helen is not quite sure, perhaps it was the articles on exercise in *Cosmo* that finally persuaded her to try it. In 1969, she began secretly exercising at home. Today, no matter where she is, at home or in a hotel, she starts her daily routine with a full hour of exercise, including 30 pushups, 120 leg kicks, and 25 deep knee bends.

A Model Wife

For a woman so focused on her career, it is sometimes hard to picture Helen Brown in her role as wife. Yet she truly follows the advice she gives in her latest book, *Having It All,* published in 1982. In it, she boasts that she gives her husband "the grade A, number one treatment, *always.*" Each morning, following her exercises, Helen cooks her husband's breakfast (and dinner in the evening if they are home). His breakfast consists of a hot cereal or grits. Hers is a concoction of a high-protein powder mixed in a blender with ginger ale, strawberries, and an artificial sweetener, 110 calories in all.

Skinny and Healthy

From her teen years to her mid-thirties, Helen spent a great deal of time in doctor's offices trying to control her weight. Because her mother had tended to be a bit plump, Helen always fretted that she would be, too. But at age thirty-six, she decided that it was not enough to diet and worry. She began a routine of "eating right" and taking vitamins.

Helen usually brings her lunch to the office in a brown paper bag. It contains such things as a special low-calorie tuna salad or plain yogurt with vegetables. As a result of eating such foods, Helen insists she has not missed a day of work in years because of illness.

Brains versus Beauty

There is no question in Helen's mind that if a mouseburger is to achieve, brains are better than beauty. Unless you want to be a model or an actress, the advantage is to the woman with brains who has an interesting personality and an upbeat manner. Nevertheless, Helen encourages all women to make the most of their looks.

In addition to exercise, a big part of Helen's morning routine includes proper care of her skin and hair, and the correct application of makeup. Then she is off to the office.

Some articles say Mrs. Brown travels to work by bus because it keeps her in touch with ordinary people. That may be true because Helen admits there is an economical streak in her. David often joshes her about her little economies, but Helen finds it hard to forget the days when she had to scrimp and save to get what she wanted.

IN THE EXECUTIVE SUITE

One of the privileges of being a chief executive is that you can set your own work schedule. Mrs. Brown is a "night person." Whereas some people do their best work early in the morning, Helen does her best later on in the day. When she worked for others, she had to conform to their schedule. Today, her secretaries and other *Cosmo* **personnel** conform to Helen's schedule. This boss arrives at her office between ten and ten-thirty in the morning.

Mrs. Brown's corner office is on the eighth floor of the Hearst headquarters on West 57th Street in the heart of New York City. There is something homey and almost old-fashioned about the large, private office. Flowered wallpaper covers the walls. The furniture is overstuffed and little square pillows adorn the sofa. One of them reads, "I LOVE CHAMPAGNE CAVIAR AND CASH." On one windowsill sits a collection of china dolls in gingham dresses. A makeup mirror hangs near her desk. Instead of a computer or an electric typewriter, an old hand-driven office typewriter sits on Mrs. Brown's desk.

People describe Helen as small and almost painfully thin. She speaks in a soft voice and manages to charm most of those who meet her.

Managing a Work Load

Much of Mrs. Brown's work in the office consists of reading and editing the articles for future issues of the magazine. Because Helen believes that no writer does their best writing the first time, eighty percent of the articles that come to *Cosmo* go back to the authors for changes.

Every Friday the staff presents a list of ideas for feature articles, to which Editor-in-Chief Brown adds her own. She and her editors work ahead on a six-month schedule. She also checks with the art department on their selection of the monthly cover. On rare occasions, Helen has to use her **veto** power and turn one down. Nothing gets by this tiny, but tough lady. She checks *every* photo and *every* word. She no longer needs David Brown to help with her daily decision-making. She now makes them promptly and on her own.

On Thursdays, Helen and the publisher invite various advertisers to lunch. One week it can be people from Revlon beauty products; another it can be advertising people for the Ford Motor Company. At such luncheons, Helen's role is to talk about the magazine, show a recent issue, and demonstrate how well *Cosmo* serves the advertiser's needs.

Helen is an extremely well-organized person and uses her time well. She will talk with a person on the telephone before granting an appointment. She would rather handle a matter by phone if it can be done. Brown also has several assistants, one who does nothing but type letters the editor-in-chief has dictated.

Mrs. Brown finds that letters often take far less time than phone conversations. She also feels strongly that people who have been kind or helpful should hear from her. Their kindnesses should never be taken for granted. So she sends out about ten thank-you letters a day.

Helen Brown's schedule is a tight one. She rarely goes out for lunch, but she does try to catch a nap on the office sofa after her lunch. As she says, "You can do that more easily if you're the boss – I try not to think about what the staff are saying beyond my closed door."

Attentive to every detail, Helen Gurley Brown checks the page lay-outs of every issue of Cosmo. *(Robert R. McElroy/Newsweek.)*

OUTSIDE OF THE COSMO OFFICE

Other obligations, travel abroad, or television appearances may break into Helen's daily routine. After the publication of *Sex and the Single Girl,* she became a familiar personality on night-time television. She has been featured on *The Tonight Show* and for three years gave advice about health, beauty, and careers on *Good Morning America.* She has also hosted her own cable television show, *View from Cosmo,* on the Lifetime Network. Because Helen is considered an authority on the career woman, she is frequently asked to speak at conferences and conventions.

When her workday is completed, Helen changes her clothes. She keeps several outfits in her office, so she is ready for any occasion. The Browns have a busy social schedule. Since David Brown is a well-known motion picture producer, they attend lots of movies. They also see plays or dine with friends. They try to keep weekends to themselves, so that they can catch their breath. Helen does not see herself as a workaholic, because she says bluntly that she loves what she is doing.

The weekends also afford time for Helen to catch up on her *Cosmo* reading and planning for the coming week. That includes jotting down memos for various staff members. By Monday morning, staff offices will be flooded with notes on pink paper. "We call it the pink hurricane, " say members of her staff.

Once a month a package arrives at the Brown apartment. It contains a future issue of the magazine. It also means that this is David's time to write the blurbs that appear on the cover of the magazine. He has discovered that the best cover blurbs include the word "you" and give advice on how the reader can feel better, or prettier, or obtain more money. David wrote blurbs when he worked for *Cosmopolitan* years ago, and he has continued to do them for Helen since she became its editor-in-chief.

LIFE AT HOME

The very successful Browns live in an elegant penthouse apartment in Manhattan, in New York City. The works of famous artists like Marc Chagall hang on the walls. Today, Helen can afford the best, and her closets are filled with clothes from expensive designers like Calvin Klein, Donna Karan, and Adolfo. She gives many of them away to the Arthritis Foundation and to people who work for her. But she hasn't forgotten the days when she used to entertain herself by trying on clothes all afternoon in chic Beverly Hills shops. She still loves to shop for bargains, even in Paris, and she still finds it hard to part with her money.

Though both Helen and David enjoy being with people, they rarely entertain at home. Helen finds she is just too busy with her work. She has neither the time nor the energy to give to entertaining and finds it takes just too much effort. As she herself explains, "The woman who has worked for me for 20 years is a darling but about parties she doesn't know."

Helen requires a full eight hours' sleep, so she is in bed by midnight most evenings. Helen admits, "Maybe if I took life more slowly I wouldn't need all that [sleep] – who knows?" But slowing down does not seem to fit into Helen Brown's life-style.

Chapter 7

A Woman of Influence

For five years (1976-1981), the *World Almanac* voted Helen Gurley Brown one of the twenty-five most influential women in the country. She has been voted one of the top ten achievers in the United States by the Women Achievers Association of America. In 1971, she received the Distinguished Achievement Award from the University of Southern California's School of Journalism and from the School of Journalism at Stanford University in 1977. In Washington, D.C., in 1972, the American Newspaper Women's Club gave Brown a special award for editorial leadership. And in 1988, Helen was inducted into the Publisher's Hall of Fame. That put her in the company of such publishing greats as Henry Luce of the Time-Life Company.

A VERY SPECIAL HONOR

One of her greatest honors was bestowed on Helen by The Hearst Corporation, owner of *Cosmopolitan* magazine. In 1985, Hearst Corporation executives funded the $300,000 Helen Gurley Brown Research Professorship at Northwestern University's Medill School of Journalism. Individuals who hold this professorship have the goal of training and interesting Medill students in the special field of magazine journalism. These professors are also responsible for starting and conducting research into the broad area of professional magazine journalism.

Helen Brown was delighted with the honor that would keep her name alive. As Helen has said:

> I didn't have any children to perpetuate my name, and I didn't go to a university myself. . . . To be able to have a chair in your name is a big, razzle-dazzle thrill. I guess you wouldn't do that for someone who was a nitwit. . . . I hope this professorship . . . will inspire and encourage young people toward a career in magazine journalism. It is a profession that is meaningful and rewarding and I would like the young people just starting out to know that.

THE MOUSEBURGER GIVES ADVICE

"If I can make it, so can you." Those words of Helen Brown sum up her attitude to those who read *Cosmo* and her books of advice to women of today. She feels strongly that if she could overcome the difficulties of being a poor girl, suffering from, as she describes it, "wall-to-wall acne" and a lack of education, others can do it as well. Her advice springs from her years of experience and her desire to share it with others. Though her advice is geared to the working woman, most of her suggestions also apply to men. Here are some of Helen's ideas.

Starting Out

1. Get started in whatever job is offered to you and hang in there, doing the best you can. Even if you have a college degree, don't turn up your nose at a secretarial job, because it is often a stepping stone to the next job.
2. Don't worry about getting to the top fast. Just plug away and do the best you can, keeping your eyes and ears open for ways to be useful to the company. Strive for excellence in whatever you do.
3. Use every opportunity to work on whatever talents you have. Make your own opportunities.

   In her book, *Having It All*, Brown describes how, as a budding copywriter she decided to give her talents a workout. Every day, she would pass a beauty shop on the way to work. The window of the shop was boring and fly-specked. She decided to type up a series of "special offers" to be put in the window that would lure passersby into the shop. The shopkeeper liked them, printed them, and reported that business had improved. Helen didn't make any money on the work but she did receive a free hairstyling and the opportunity to practice her talent successfully.

4. There is no way to succeed without putting in the long hours and the drudgery. If you work hard, the hard work rewards you.
5. Don't worry about competition. You are really only competing against yourself.
6. Don't be stingy with your time, even if that means working overtime or on Saturdays. Nice people finish first!
7. Do what you are expected to do *this minute* . . . or at least this day. Get back to people promptly.

Along the Way

8. You may be very aggressive on the inside, but don't let it show.
9. Getting along well with people is at least fifty percent of success, but that doesn't mean you have to be popular or an office clown.
10. Dress well for the office.
11. If you don't know what somebody is talking about, don't be afraid to ask questions.
12. Don't hesitate to ask for help or to borrow ideas from others. They should be able to do the same with you.
13. Make your boss look good.
14. Praise those who work for you and give them credit when they deserve it.
15. Never lose your temper.

16. As you begin to gain success, don't brag and don't expect others to tell you that you're wonderful. If you're good, you don't need to brag.

THE PERKS OF SUCCESS

Looking back at her achievements, Helen Gurley Brown is thoroughly delighted with the life she has led and is still leading. Her name is a **byword** in the publishing field. She and her husband lead the kind of exciting life that she could only dream of when she was starting out. They have met and become friends with people from all walks of life, such as Irving Berlin, the great composer of popular music; Richard Nixon, former President of the United States; singer and actor Frank Sinatra; Henry Kissinger, former secretary of state; and oil magnate Jean Paul Getty, once one of the richest men in the world.

Most people find themselves very attracted to Helen and David Brown. He is a natural storyteller. His latest book, *Let Me Entertain You,* is filled with amusing incidents about people he has met in his interesting career as writer, editor, and Hollywood producer. As for Helen, she is a marvelous listener. People who have interviewed her say that she listens intently and gazes into the interviewer's eyes. She tends to emphasize her stories with a gentle hand on the interviewer's shoulders or arm. It is a technique she suggests in *Cosmo* articles, but it seems to come naturally to her.

Pet Peeves and Adventures

Despite the charm that she displays, Helen admits that she has several pet peeves. One is head waiters who are too stuffy or act as if they are doing you a favor. She is also irritated by people who can't finish a phone conversation quickly or who spend most of the time talking about themselves. She often gets so upset when caught with people like this at a dinner that she will pick up a spoon and bend it with her hands. David has learned to make an excuse and a hasty exit when he sees a bent spoon in Helen's hands.

Between David's work and her own, the Browns have had a wealth of adventures and, whenever possible, they share them. They have been interviewed by Barbara Walters for the television show "20/20." They have served as lecturers on the great English ocean liner, the *Queen Elizabeth II* (or the QE2), while sailing down the coast of East Africa. Their travels have taken them to Turkey, Egypt, Israel, Botswana, South Africa, China, Morocco, all of Western Europe, and China.

PLANS FOR THE FUTURE

Most people retire by age sixty-five, and most of the publishing industry expected Helen Brown to do just that. But she has passed that landmark birthday and is still going strong. Why does Helen continue to thrive on a schedule that would have a person twenty years younger than she is gasping for breath?

Going strong into the 1990s at the helm of Cosmopolitan *magazine, Helen Gurley Brown still uses her old manual typewriter at work.* (Cosmopolitan *magazine.*)

The biggest reason is that she loves her work. In an article celebrating the twenty-fifth anniversary of her appointment at *Cosmopolitan*, Helen told a reporter, "Work is a real, real confidence booster. I've always found that work works. . . . Whatever you put into work you get back, mostly." She feels a big part of her job is to instill that kind of confidence in the women who read *Cosmo*.

Besides, Mrs. Brown believes, "Being too busy is a very good way not to think about yourself." With a workday of ten, eleven, or twelve hours, one has to believe that Helen means it. In addition to her *Cosmo* chores, she is presently working on another book.

The Best Thing about Success

Is Helen pleased with her fame and fortune? In a recent interview she gave her thoughts on that subject.

> The best thing about my success is knowing that I did it. I took an idea and made something of it. I'm a good magazine editor and I'm highly paid for it. . . . I'm not Cher, I'm not Madonna, but I'm famous enough that people know me – and most even like me.

The Hearst Corporation is a privately owned company without a required retirement date. According to her contract, Helen can stay on the job as long as *Cosmo's* profits continue to climb. Then why doesn't she slow down a bit? Why doesn't she take more time to relax with her husband and friends? Why doesn't she talk about retiring?

Friends who know her well say it is because down deep Helen is still a barefoot girl from Arkansas who gets up every morning afraid she's going to be fired. Brown herself admits that this is true. She can't stop being a workaholic "because I'm scared my laurels [honors] would disappear beneath me."

Helen is a natural-born worrier. She worries about money, even though there is no need to, and she worries about growing old. She also worries about her husband, who would rather smoke cigars and work than exercise.

Helen is someone who prides herself on staying in shape and looking as young as possible. She admits to being "a health nut." She also admits that it took her a while to recover when a young woman in a bus got up to give her a seat.

Once, when asked what her attitude toward life is, Helen replied, "Say yes to everything and keep saying yes as long as you can."

Glossary

administrator   One who performs management duties.

blurb   A short, public notice.

byword   A word or saying that represents a particular type of person or thing.

circulation   The average number of copies of a publication sold over a given period of time.

copywriter   One who writes the short messages used in advertisements.

editor   One who prepares copy for publication.

employee   One who is hired to work for another for wages.

finance   The management of money by a government, business, or individual.

Great Depression   A period during the 1930s marked by serious unemployment and a severe drop in business activity.

hardcover   An edition of a book produced with a more expensive, firm cover as opposed to a soft cover or paperback edition.

marketing   The process of selling a product or service for a company.

negotiate   To confer with others so as to arrive at the settlement of some matter.

niche   A place, employment, or activity for which a person is best suited.

personnel   A group of people employed in a factory, office, or organization.

philosophy   The beliefs, ideas, and attitudes of an individual or a group.

press release   Material given in advance to newspapers, magazines, radio, or television for something to be announced later.

prospectus   A preliminary statement that describes a business and is distributed to possible buyers or investors.

publisher   One who prints and offers for sale books or other printed matter.

revenue   The income that comes back from an investment.

syndicate   A business concern that sells materials for publication to a number of newspapers or magazines.

veto   To refuse to approve something.

workaholic   A person who works very long hours and prefers this to recreation or play.

Index